Turning Points in World History

Happy House

About Wise & Wide

- A systematic 6-level English reading program based on Lexile® measures
- Diverse and interesting topics chosen from the elementary curriculums of Korea and English speaking western countries
- Well-written books in various forms including fiction stories, descriptive texts, and classics retold
- The informative but original fiction stories grab your interest, leading to the easy and clear understanding of the educational content.
- Improve thinking skills with solid after-reading activities at all levels of the series.

Wise & Wide is a 6-level English reading program that consists of 60 books and each level is systematically divided by Lexile® measures. The Lexile® Framework for Reading is the most popular reading measuring system in American formal education curriculums and many English programs. Over 20 out of 50 states in the U.S. mark Lexile® measures directly on students' final report cards and over 300 well-known publishers adopt and use Lexile® measures.

Experience many kinds of readings written by professional writers from the U.S. and England. They used interesting topics that were carefully chosen after analyzing elementary curriculums from around the world including Korea, the U.S., England, and Australia among many others. Comprehensive after-reading activities including graphic organizers, speaking tasks, and After-reading Tests are ready for you.

Levels in the series and their corresponding Lexile® measures

Level	Lexile® measures	U.S. Grade
Level 1	Below 200L	Pre K - K
Level 2	190L - 400L	Lower Grade 1
Level 3	350L - 530L	Upper Grade 1
Level 4	420L - 650L	Grade 2
Level 5	520L - 940L	Grade 3 - 4
Level 6	830L - 1070L	Grade 5 - 6

* Smart Readers: Wise & Wide level 1 is applicable to the preschool level in the U.S.
* The source of the relationship between Lexile® measures and U.S. school grades: CCSS(Common Core State Standards) FOR ENGLISH LANGUAGE ARTS, APPENDIX A (2012, which is used by 45 states in the U.S.)

Topic List

	Level 1	Level 2	Level 3	Level 4	Level 5	Level 6
Book 1	Science>Biology: The hibernation of animals Story	Science>Biology: Living and nonliving things Story	Science>Biology> Animals & the Environment: Sea otters Story	Environment> Living with nature: The diver & the persimmon tree Story	Science>Biology> Animal: Amazing animals of the Amazon Story	Science>Biology: Germs, transmitted diseases Story
Book 2	Literature> World classics: Aesop's fables Story	Literature> Traditional fairy tale: Old tales about stones Story	Social Studies> Economy: To run a business to make and save money Story	Science>Biology> Plants: Photosynthesis Story	Science>Earth science: Earth's layers, earthquakes, volcanoes, and earth's atmosphere Report	Mathematics> Sequence: The golden ratio & the Fibonacci sequence Story
Book 3	Science>Physics: How shadows are formed Story	Literature> World classics: Peter Pan Story	Science>Scientific technology: Nanobots Story	Literature>Myths: World's creation stories Story	Literature> Legend: The story of King Arthur Story	Literature>Myths: Constellation myths Story
Book 4	Literature> Traditional literature: The Talmud Story	Science>Biology> Animal: Polar bears Story	Science>Biology> Animal: Mountain gorillas Story	Social Studies> Cultural anthropology: Amazing ancient cultures of the world Story	Science> Earth science: Clouds and weather Story	Literature> Human & animals: The friendship between a girl and a horse Story
Book 5	Social Studies> Ethics: Rules in daily life Story	Science>Biology: The five senses Report	Social Studies> Cultural anthropology: Astonishing festivals Report	Art>Music: Stories from two operas Story	Social Studies> World culture & history: The Renaissance Story	Sports> Board sports: Surfing & snowboarding Story
Book 6	Social Studies> World geography & travel: Tourist attractions around the world Story	Science>Biology> Animal: Dinosaurs Story	Science> Astronomy: The solar system Story	Social Studies> People: Three great people who overcame hardships Story	Science>Scientific technology: The wonderful world of robots Report	Art>Music: Composers of the Romantic Era Report
Book 7	Science> Space science: The life of astronauts Report	Social Studies> Cultural anthropology: Mythological monsters from around the world Report	Mathematics> Elementary mathematics: Numbers, measurement, shapes and data Report	Science & Social Studies> Technology & culture: Inventions from around the world Report	Art>Works of art: Famous paintings Report	Social Studies> Human & animals: Animals in action for human Report
Book 8	Social Studies> Cultural anthropology: Various living cultures of the world Story	Art>Music: Instruments in the orchestra Story	Social Studies> Life safety: Learning and using outdoor survival skills Story	Social Studies> History: The California Gold Rush Report	Social Studies & Science> Psychology: Psychology in everyday life Story	Literature> World classics: The Merchant of Venice Story
Book 9	Social Studies> Jobs: Interviews about jobs Report	Science>Scientific technology: Developments in technology in different times Story	Social Studies> Politics>Election: Running for 3rd grade class president Story	Literature> World classics: Stories of Sherlock Holmes Story	Literature> World classics: Adrift in the Pacific Story	Social Studies> History & People: Great world leaders in history Report
Book 10	Literature>Traditional fairy tale: Eastern and Western folk tales on the same theme Story	Sports>Winter sports: Various aspects of some Winter Olympic sports Report	Literature> World classics: Short stories by O. Henry Story	Sports> Ball games: Various aspects of popular ball games Report	Social Studies> History: Famous events that changed world history Report	Art & Social Studies> Art: Stories about the creation, distribution, and preservation of paintings Report

How to Use
This Book

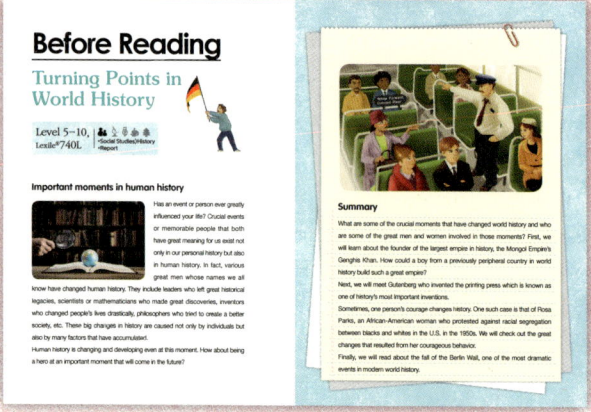

•Before Reading

You can easily find the topic and what kind of story you are about to read.

•The text

All the stories were written by professional writers from the U.S. and England, so you will read authentic and appropriate English sentences and expressions in every book in the series.

•Pop Quiz

Check out right away if you understand what you have just read by solving a pop quiz that checks your comprehension.

•Key Words

The key words and expressions on each page are listed for you to easily study them.

•Aha! Tips

Download free Korean explanations at *www.ihappyhouse.co.kr* for all of the sentences marked with "Aha!". These explain cultural scientific, and economic knowledge or they deal with aspects of English such as grammatical structures or idiomatic expressions. There are lots of "Aha! Tips" to help you understand the text.

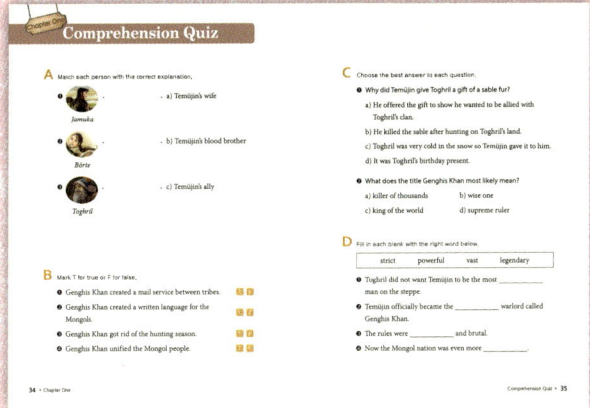

•Comprehension Quiz

After reading one chapter, solve various questions to find out if you fully understand the content.

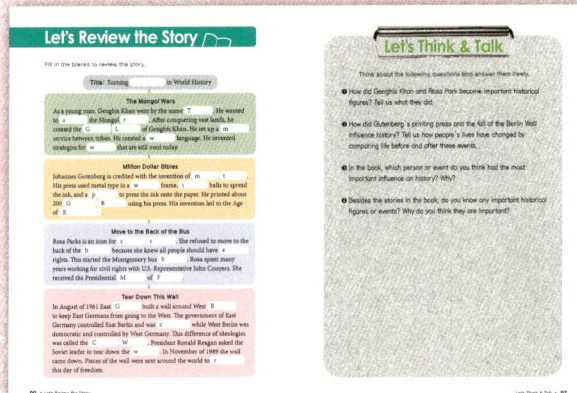

•Let's Review the Story /
•Let's Think & Talk

Fill in the blanks in the organizer to summarize the whole story. Express your own thinking and feelings about the story by answering the questions. You can build up logic and reasoning skills for your essay examinations in the future.

Appendix

Audio CD
In the CD audio book form, the texts are read vividly by American professional voice actors. (MP3 files downloaded for free)

After-reading Test
Solve an additionally provided After-reading Test for each book.

The Korean translation, Answer Keys, a Word Quiz, a Word List, and Aha! Tips for each book
You can download them for free at *www.ihappyhouse.co.kr* or *www.darakwon.co.kr*

Before Reading

Turning Points in World History

Level 5–10, Lexile®740L

- Social Studies>History
- Report

Important moments in human history

Has an event or person ever greatly influenced your life? Crucial events or memorable people that both have great meaning for us exist not only in our personal history but also in human history. In fact, various great men whose names we all know have changed human history. They include leaders who left great historical legacies, scientists or mathematicians who made great discoveries, inventors who changed people's lives drastically, philosophers who tried to create a better society, etc. These big changes in history are caused not only by individuals but also by many factors that have accumulated.

Human history is changing and developing even at this moment. How about being a hero at an important moment that will come in the future?

Summary

What are some of the crucial moments that have changed world history and who are some of the great men and women involved in those moments? First, we will learn about the founder of the largest empire in history, the Mongol Empire's Genghis Khan. How could a boy from a previously peripheral country in world history build such a great empire?

Next, we will meet Gutenberg who invented the printing press which is known as one of history's most important inventions.

Sometimes, one person's courage changes history. One such case is that of Rosa Parks, an African-American woman who protested against racial segregation between blacks and whites in the U.S. in the 1950s. We will check out the great changes that resulted from her courageous behavior.

Finally, we will read about the fall of the Berlin Wall, one of the most dramatic events in modern world history.

Contents

Turning Points in World History

Turning Points in
World History

The Mongol Wars

Horse hooves thundered across the snowy steppes, or grasslands, carrying Mongol soldiers with swords, knives, and arrows. Aha! The Jin Dynasty emperor had killed a Mongol messenger. Genghis Khan had sent a message to the emperor calling him a coward. This meant war!

The generals under Genghis Khan led the way into the battle. They surrounded the enemy. The Jin soldiers thought they were better than the Mongol army. They should not have been so sure.

▲ steppe

KEY WORDS

- hoof
- thunder
- steppe (*cf.* the Steppes)
- grassland
- carry
- sword
- arrow
- Jin Dynasty (*cf.* dynasty)

- emperor (*cf.* empress)
- coward
- mean (mean-meant-meant)
- general
- lead the way (lead-led-led)
- surround
- should have + *p.p.*

Mongol soldiers shot arrows into the Jin army. They killed men and horses. When they finished shooting, they rode away. The Jin army thought they had time to rest. But they were wrong. Right behind the first wave of Mongol soldiers came another wave of soldiers. They shot and killed many more.

Now the Jin army was afraid. They knew firsthand why the Mongol soldiers were the most feared in all the world. The Jin soldiers tried to run away. But there was nowhere to run. The Mongol army continued shooting arrows at the Jin soldiers. The survivors were wounded and weak, but they did not surrender. Finally, the Mongol army charged in and killed them all with swords and more arrows. After the 1211 Battle of Yehuling, the emperor was killed by one of his own generals. This was the beginning of the end of the Jin Dynasty in China. It was also one of the last war campaigns for the great Genghis Khan.

POP QUIZ

Who was the Mongol army fighting against?

ⓐ the Jin Dynasty soldiers
ⓑ the great Genghis Khan

KEY WORDS

- **shoot** (shoot-shot-shot)
- **ride away** (ride-rode-ridden)
- rest
- wrong
- wave
- afraid
- firsthand
- feared
- **run away** (run-ran-run)
- nowhere
- survivor
- **wounded** (= injured)
- surrender
- charge
- campaign

Early Years of Genghis Khan

▲ (See page for author [Public domain], via Wikimedia Commons)

Battles among the tribes of the Mongolian steppes, or grasslands, were a way of life when the boy named Temüjin was born. This was the name Genghis Khan used when he was young. The tribes were constantly at war. If someone wronged another person in a different tribe, it was never forgotten. Even years later, they could be attacked in revenge.

Temüjin wanted a different future for the people of the steppes. He wanted to unite the tribes.

KEY WORDS

- tribe
- name
- constantly
- at war
- **forget** (forget-forgot-forgotten)

- even
- attack
- in revenge
- unite

But Temüjin the boy had a hard life. Like all children of the steppes, he learned to ride a horse and shoot a bow and arrow as soon as his legs were long enough to reach the stirrups! Aha!

As a result he could hunt and fight in battles from a very young age. When Temüjin was eight or nine years old, his father was poisoned by a member of a clan of Tatars. Once Temüjin's father was dead, he and his family were cast out of their own clan. This was because his mother was an outsider. His family traveled alone. Sometimes they camped near other clans.

KEY WORDS

- bow
- as soon as
- enough
- stirrup
- as a result
- poison
- clan

- once
- cast out (cast-cast-cast)
- outsider
- travel
- sometimes
- camp

A boy named Jamuka lived in one of those clans. Temüjin and Jamuka played together and became best friends. Their friendship was so strong, that one day, they cut their hands with arrowheads and became *andas*, or blood brothers.

On the steppes, when a father dies, the oldest son becomes the leader of the family. In Temüjin's family, this was Begter. Begter treated Temüjin badly. One day Temüjin finally had enough. He shot Begter with an arrow and left him to die. This act did not go unpunished. Temüjin's old clan, the same one that had cast him out when his father died, came back and took him prisoner. They tied him to an animal yoke and made him a slave.

From this, Temüjin learned never to trust people completely, even his friends and allies. It only caused him pain.

One night he escaped. A farmer helped him by giving him a horse. He rode out onto the steppes and began a new life. He used his skills in fighting and hunting to survive and build his own tribe.

POP QUIZ

Who helped Temüjin escape from slavery?
ⓐ a farmer
ⓑ a farmer's wife

KEY WORDS

- friendship
- arrowhead
- blood brother
- treat (*cf.* treatment)
- go unpunished (go-went-gone)
- take prisoner (take-took-taken)(*cf.* prisoner)

- yoke
- slave
- trust
- ally
- cause
- pain

When he was sixteen, Temüjin married Börte. Her father gave them a valuable sable fur as a wedding gift.

Temüjin wanted to become an ally with the powerful tribe called Kereit. 📖 Toghril, the leader of this tribe had been *andas*, or blood brothers, with Temüjin's father. Temüjin gave Toghril the sable fur and told him he would fight for his tribe whenever it was needed. In return, Toghril promised to protect Temüjin and his tribe. Temüjin made new friends who would later become powerful allies.

Soon after this, Börte was kidnapped by the Merkit tribe. Toghril and Jamuka sent 40,000 men to get her back. They surrounded the small village shouting war cries.

"I am Temüjin!" shouted the man on the biggest horse. "I am here for my wife, Börte!"

KEY WORDS

- valuable
- sable
- whenever
- in return
- kidnap
- get back (get-got-gotten)
- war cry

All at once, arrows flew through the air. Several wounded men fell to the frozen ground. Temüjin leaped off his horse. He called

to Börte and she raced to his arms. He lifted her over his broad shoulders and ran back to his horse. Börte held on tight as Temüjin and his men raced around the settlement, killing the Merkits. They also brought back horses and golden sashes.

Once they got back to Temüjin's camp, a big feast was prepared to celebrate the victory and to welcome Börte home.

KEY WORDS

- all at once
- frozen
- **leap off** (*cf.* leap)
- race
- broad
- **hold on tight** (hold-held-held)(*cf.* tight)

- settlement
- sash
- feast
- prepare
- celebrate
- welcome

"Vengeance is mine!" shouted Temüjin as he stood beside the roaring bonfire. "I have exacted justice upon my enemy! May all who hear of this bow in fear of my strength!"

The men and their families cheered Temüjin and their tribe as they ate and drank.

Later, Temüjin would climb to the top of Burkhan Khaldun, or God Mountain. There he would sprinkle goat's milk and pray to the spirits of the earth, sun and sky.

Soon after, Börte had a baby. Temüjin named him Jochi. He was the first-born son.

KEY WORDS

- vengeance
- roaring
- bonfire
- exact
- justice
- may
- hear of
- in fear of
- strength
- cheer
- sprinkle
- pray
- spirit
- have a baby (have-had-had)

Jamuka and Temüjin fought side by side and stayed friends for a long time.

In 1189, Temüjin was named leader of the Mongols. This made Jamuka very angry. He wanted to be the leader. He attacked Temüjin's tribe. He boiled some of Temüjin's men alive. Temüjin vowed to take revenge.

Over the years, as he conquered other tribes, he did something new. Instead of making the people prisoners and slaves, he welcomed them into his tribe if they would give him their loyalty. If they resisted, they were killed. But if they agreed to side with Temüjin, he let them live. No Mongol leader had ever done this before.

POP QUIZ

What new thing did Temüjin do with prisoners?
ⓐ He allowed his prisoners to live if they declared loyalty to him.
ⓑ He made them all slaves.

KEY WORDS

- side by side
- boil
- vow
- take revenge
- conquer
- instead of

- loyalty
- resist
- agree
- side with
- lay down (lay-laid-laid)
- loot

- divide
- fairly
- receive
- fair
- portion
- respect

He did another new thing when he went to fight the Tatars in
the year 1201. Before the battle, Temüjin laid down new laws.
Temüjin said that all the loot from the battle would be given to
him. He would divide it fairly among his soldiers. The families of
any soldiers killed would also receive a fair portion. This made
the people trust and respect him.

By now Temüjin had vast armies of soldiers. He knew he had to organize his armies to be efficient and strong. He used the decimal number system to do this. 🌐 A squad had ten men, a company had one hundred, and a battalion had one thousand. Each of these had leaders chosen by the soldiers. A *tumen* had ten thousand soldiers. Temüjin chose the leaders of each *tumen*. They reported directly to Temüjin. Now he only had to give an order to these top men, and it was quickly followed by tens of thousands of soldiers.

KEY WORDS

- by now
- vast
- organize
- efficient
- decimal number (*cf.* decimal)
- squad
- company
- battalion
- report
- directly
- only have to + *Verb*
- give an order (give-gave-given)

- follow
- tens of thousands
- commander
- increase
- sneak
- faithful
- shepherd
- warn of
- catch (catch-caught-caught)
- troops
- by surprise

Soon Temüjin was the commander of eighty thousand men.
He sent a message to Toghril, asking if his first-born son Jochi
could marry one of Toghril's daughters. This would increase the
power of both men. Toghril agreed and they made plans to meet
on the steppes.

But Toghril planned a sneak attack on Temüjin's armies. He did
not want Temüjin to be the most powerful man on the steppes.
A faithful shepherd warned Temüjin of the attack. Temüjin and
his men rode quickly and caught Toghril's troops by surprise.
Toghril was killed when he tried to escape.

But Jamuka's armies were also waiting to kill Temüjin. So Temüjin had each of his men light five campfires. In the dark, it would seem as if Temüjin had five times more men than he really had.

▲ tumbleweed

He attacked before sunrise from many different directions. He called this the "tumbleweed formation." In the morning, he had rows and rows of soldiers advance. Each row of soldiers would shoot at Jamuka's army, then the next row would shoot. This was called the "lake formation." The rows of men did not stop, just like waves on a lake. Most of Jamuka's soldiers were killed.

Temüjin created many other war strategies like these. 🌐 Some commanders still use them today.

▲ the Caracole Tactic,
one of the most notable Mongol military tactics

Jamuka and the last of his soldiers escaped into the forest. Some of his soldiers surrendered to Temüjin. They told him where Jamuka was hiding. Temüjin took Jamuka prisoner. Then, because he thought Jamuka's men

were cowards, he had them all killed. Jamuka asked Temüjin to kill him too, and bury his body. He told Temüjin he would watch over him in death. Temüjin granted his wish.

KEY WORDS

- light (light-lit-lit)
- as if
- tumbleweed
- formation
- row

- advance
- strategy
- escape
- hide (hide-hid-hidden)
- bury

- watch over
- grant
- wish

A New Name for Temüjin

One year later, in 1206, in a large meeting of the Mongols on the Onon River, the people gave Temüjin a new name. He officially became the legendary warlord called Genghis Khan. Khan means ruler. Historians are not sure what the name Genghis means. Some say it means "oceans." Some say it means "supreme." So, we might say Genghis Khan means "Supreme Ruler." It was a fitting name.

By now, Genghis Khan had an empire that stretched over thousands of miles. He named the more than one million people living in his empire the Great Mongol Nation.

KEY WORDS

- officially
- legendary
- warlord
- ruler

- historian
- supreme
- fitting
- empire

- stretch
- nation

He also created the Great Law of Genghis Khan. It was a code of laws. His laws were higher than all the local tribal laws. Most offenses were punishable by death. If a person lied, or stole property, or kidnapped someone, he was killed. The rules were strict and brutal.

Genghis Khan also did many good things for his people. He set up a mail service between tribes. There was a postal station with delivery by horse about every twenty miles. He set up a hunting season so baby animals had time to grow. He also created a written language for the Mongols. 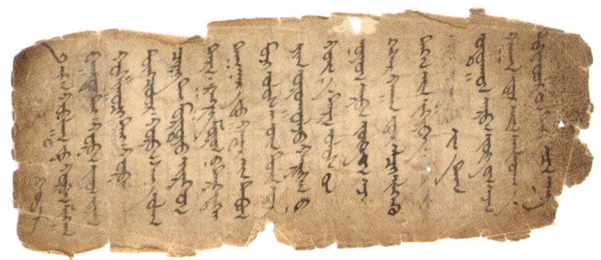 His victories in battles increased the possessions of the Mongol tribes.

▲ ancient mogolian script(Writing runs top to bottom, left to right.)

KEY WORDS

- **code of laws** (*cf.* code)
- **tribal**
- **offense**
- **punishable**
- **lie** (lie-lied-lied)

- **steal** (steal-stole-stolen)
- **property**
- **rule**
- **brutal**
- **set up** (set-set-set)

- **mail service**
- **postal station**
- **delivery**
- **written language**
- **possession**

Even after all of this, Genghis Khan was not satisfied. In 1211, during the Jin Dynasty, 65,000 Mongol soldiers crossed the Gobi Desert into China and attacked. They tricked people into opening the city gates. The soldiers would drop supplies and ride away. The people thought the army had retreated. They opened their gates to get the supplies and were attacked by the returning Mongol soldiers.

KEY WORDS
- satisfied
- trick into
- supply
- retreat

By 1215, the Great Mongol Nation had many riches. Genghis Khan wanted to open up trade with the Muslim city of Khwarizm. He sent a message to Sultan Mohammed II, telling him he did not want war, but wanted to trade riches with them. He sent a caravan to the city of Otrar, full of gold, silver, and jade. The governor of the city had the people in the caravan killed. Genghis Khan sent ambassadors to Sultan Mohammed II. They demanded an apology. The sultan killed them, too! In revenge, Genghis Khan rode to Khwarizm with 100,000 men and took over the sultan's empire. Now the Mongol nation was even more vast.

KEY WORDS

- riches
- open up
- trade
- sultan
- caravan
- jade
- governor
- ambassador
- demand
- apology
- take over

But Genghis Khan was getting old. He knew his days were numbered, so he divided his empire among his and Börte's sons. He named his son Ögödei as the next khan. Historians think he chose Ögödei as his successor because he was a good negotiator.

In 1226, on a trip to China, Genghis Khan was thrown from a horse and injured. He died six months later. His burial site was kept secret for over 800 years.

KEY WORDS

- someone[something]'s days are numbered
- successor
- negotiator
- on a trip to

- throw (throw-threw-thrown)
- burial
- site
- keep secret (keep-kept-kept)

After his death, the sons and grandsons of Genghis Khan increased the Great Mongol Nation until it covered nearly one fourth of the continent of Asia!  Aha!

Today, he is known as a great leader. Even though he was a brutal warrior and enforced his laws with an iron fist, he also provided many good things for his people. He brought people from many tribes together under his rule. He created a new way of ruling that allowed people of different tribes and cultures to live together in harmony. He accomplished his dream of uniting the tribes of the steppes.

KEY WORDS

- nearly
- continent
- be known as
- even though
- warrior
- enforce

- iron fist (= iron hand)
- provide
- bring together (bring-brought-brought)
- allow
- in harmony
- accomplish

Comprehension Quiz

A Match each person with the correct explanation.

1

Jamuka

a) Temüjin's wife

2

Börte

b) Temüjin's blood brother

3

Toghril

c) Temüjin's ally

B Mark T for true or F for false.

1 Genghis Khan created a mail service between tribes.　　T　F

2 Genghis Khan created a written language for the
Mongols.　　T　F

3 Genghis Khan got rid of the hunting season.　　T　F

4 Genghis Khan unified the Mongol people.　　T　F

C Choose the best answer to each question.

❶ Why did Temüjin give Toghril a gift of a sable fur?

a) He offered the gift to show he wanted to be allied with Toghril's clan.

b) He killed the sable after hunting on Toghril's land.

c) Toghril was very cold in the snow so Temüjin gave it to him.

d) It was Toghril's birthday present.

❷ What does the title Genghis Khan most likely mean?

a) killer of thousands   b) wise one

c) king of the world   d) supreme ruler

D Fill in each blank with the right word below.

strict	powerful	vast	legendary

❶ Toghril did not want Temüjin to be the most _____ man on the steppe.

❷ Temüjin officially became the _____ warlord called Genghis Khan.

❸ The rules were _____ and brutal.

❹ Now the Mongol nation was even more _____.

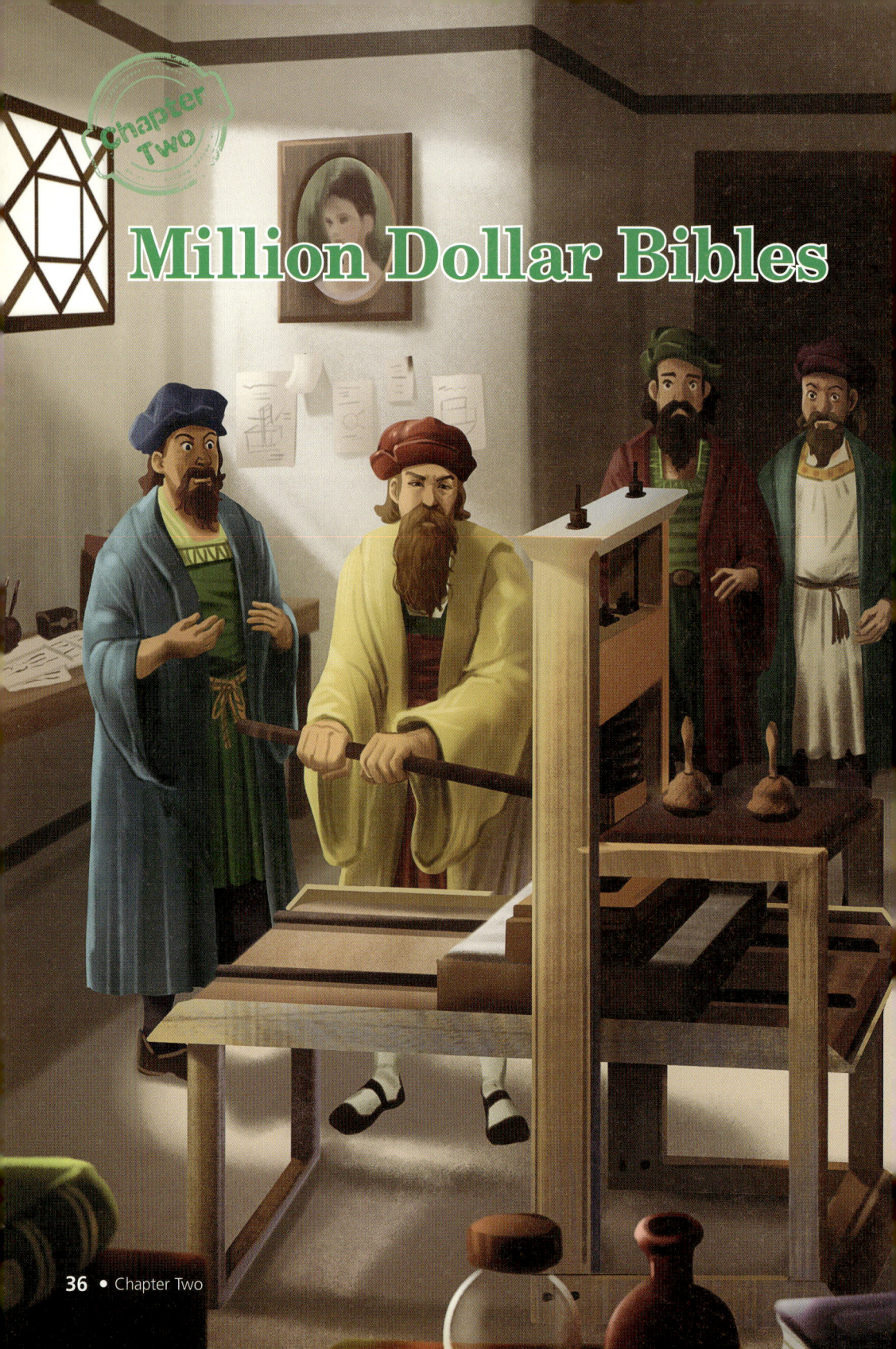

Million Dollar Bibles

In a dark room, with only one small window for light, several men watched as Johannes placed tiny metal pieces into a wooden frame. After they were in place, he used two round ink balls to pat oily, black ink over the tops of the metal pieces. He carefully placed a piece of paper on a flat surface.

Then he closed a frame over the paper to hold it in place. He carefully folded the frame down over the inked metal pieces. After that, he rolled the paper in the frame under a block of wood called a platen. With two hands he pulled a lever that turned a large wooden screw. The platen pressed down on the paper and metal. Then he rolled the paper frame out again. As he lifted the frame, the men around him were silent. They held their breath as they waited.

POP QUIZ

What did Johannes do with two round ink balls?

ⓐ He placed a piece of paper on them.
ⓑ He patted black ink over the tops of the metal pieces.

KEY WORDS

- place
- in place
- ink ball
- pat
- oily

- surface
- fold
- roll
- block
- platen

- lever
- screw
- press down on (cf. press)
- hold one's breath

When the paper frame pulled away from the metal plates, it made a sound like a kiss. Everyone leaned in close to see the paper as Johannes opened the frame. He lifted the paper with the wet ink and held it up for all to see in the light streaming in the window. The men in the room cheered and clapped. Gutenberg had just printed a German poem with his new invention, the Gutenberg Press! He thought he was simply creating a faster way to print. But his invention changed the history of the world.

Gutenberg's Beginnings

Gutenberg was born in Mainz, Germany about the year 1398. His family was wealthy, and his father worked for the church mint. He was a goldsmith who pressed coins.

Johannes learned the trade of goldsmithing from his father. From a very early age, Gutenberg worked with many different types of metal.

Around 1411, Gutenberg's family moved to Strasbourg. He finished school there. In 1448 he returned to Mainz. He took out a loan to buy the things he needed to build a printing press and set up his business.

By 1450, he was printing with his new Gutenberg Press.

KEY WORDS

- plate
- lean
- stream
- clap

- poem
- invention
- wealthy
- mint

- goldsmith (*cf.* smith)
- type
- take out a loan
- printing press (*cf.* print)

▲ movable type

The Gutenberg Press used a new technique called movable type. It made it possible to mass produce books. It could print thousands of pages a day.

How did Gutenberg come up with this idea for printing with movable type? No one knows for certain. Gutenberg kept his idea a secret until he began printing with it. But it is known that there was similar typesetting in Korea and China more than 200 years before Gutenberg's invention.

However, Gutenberg is credited with inventing a new technique and introducing the printing technology to Europe.

KEY WORDS

- **movable type** (*cf.* movable)
- **mass produce**
- **come up with** (come-came-come)
- for certain
- typesetting
- be credited with

His invention of the printing press with movable type was the beginning of the spread of knowledge during the European Renaissance. 🌐 Before this, books were made by hand. One way to print a book was with woodcarvings. Someone had to carve each page of a book into a block of wood. Then the block of wood was covered in ink and a paper laid over it. This type of printing was very slow.

KEY WORDS

- **spread** (spread-spread-spread)
- **knowledge**
- **the Renaissance**
- **woodcarving**
- **carve**
- **lay over** (lay-laid-laid)

Other books were copied by hand. 🌐 Priests or monks would do the copying and illustrating. You can imagine that it could take up to a year to copy and illustrate one book. Both these ways made books very expensive. Most people could never afford to buy a book, so many people never bothered to learn to read.

By the 1500s, the new printing press had spread like wildfire all over Europe. People could print identical books and distribute them everywhere.

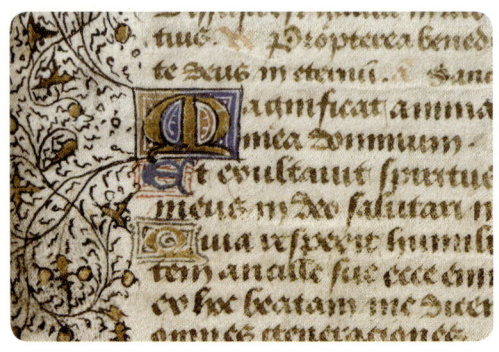

▲ an illuminated manuscript

The First Printed Bibles

Around 1455 Johannes printed almost 200 copies of what we call the Gutenberg Bible. Most pages of the bible had 42 lines, making them have the same format on all the pages.

▲ (By NYC Wanderer (Kevin Eng) (originally posted to Flickr as Gutenberg Bible) [CC BY-SA 2.0 (http://creativecommons.org/licenses/by-sa/2.0)], via Wikimedia Commons)

He set up the type with block printing, meaning that the margins were straight and the same size. Some were printed on paper and some on vellum, which is animal skin.

KEY WORDS

- copy
- priest
- monk
- illustrate
- up to
- afford to + *Verb*
- bother
- wildfire

- identical
- distribute
- what we call (= what is called)
- line
- format
- margin
- straight
- vellum

Once a page had been printed, it was hung up to let the ink dry. Then someone called an illuminator would illustrate the pages and the letters in drop case. Drop case is the appearance of a large letter at the beginning of a section. The pages were sewn together in sections called folios. Then the folios were bound together into book form.

▲ illustrations in the Gutenberg Bible

(Andreagrossmann[Public domain],
via Wikimedia Commons)

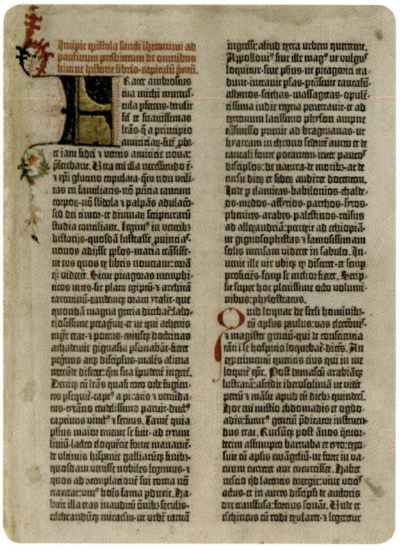

▲ drop cases in the Gutenberg Bible

(By Johannes Gutenberg [Public domain],
via Wikimedia Commons)

KEY WORDS

- **hang up** (hang-hung-hung)
- **illuminator**
- **appearance**
- **section**

- **sew** (sew-sewed-sewed/sewn)
- **folio**
- **bind** (bind-bound-bound)

Gutenberg sold his bibles for 30 florins each.  This was about the amount of money a clerk could make in three years. Even so, all the Gutenberg Bibles were sold before he even began printing.

▲ florins

Gutenberg Bibles are prized documents. Even one folio or one page can be worth millions of dollars. Today the Gutenberg Bibles or parts of them are kept in museums and university libraries. They are a beautiful testament to this period in European history.

POP QUIZ

How long did it take Gutenberg to sell all of his bibles?

ⓐ About two years.
ⓑ They were sold out before he began printing.

KEY WORDS

- florin
- amount
- clerk

- even so
- prized
- document

- worth
- testament
- period

Later, Gutenberg printed other pamphlets and papers for the church. He even printed Latin grammar schoolbooks!

In 1462, when Gutenberg was an old man, he had a dispute with an archbishop of the church. He was forced to leave Mainz again. But a few years later, he was recognized for his accomplishments. He was awarded with money, food, clothing, and wine. When he died, his body was buried in Mainz. Later, the cemetery was destroyed, and his grave was lost.

No one is certain exactly how Johannes Gutenberg made his first movable type. But what they are certain of is that his invention changed the world. For the first time in history, people all over Europe could learn to read. For the first time, individuals could buy books. For the first time, knowledge and information was available to everyone. People all over Europe began printing all types of literature, spreading new ideas and new ways of thinking. Without the Gutenberg Press, we would have never had the Scientific Revolution, the Reformation, or the Age of Enlightenment. 🌐

KEY WORDS

- pamphlet
- grammar
- dispute
- archbishop
- be forced to + *Verb*
- recognize
- accomplishment
- award
- cemetery
- destroy

- grave
- exactly
- for the first time
- individual
- available
- literature
- without
- the Scientific Revolution
- the Reformation
- the Age of Enlightenment

Comprehension Quiz

A Fill in each blank with the right word below.

leaned	died	held	illustrate

❶ They _____ their breath as they waited.

❷ Everyone _____ in close to see the paper as Johannes opened the frame.

❸ Then someone called an illuminator would _____ the pages and the letters in drop case.

❹ When he _____, his body was buried in Mainz.

B It is about how the Gutenberg Press works. Put the sentences in order.

❶ Turn the screw to lower the platen onto the paper and type.

❷ Use ink balls to spread ink over the top of the metal type.

❸ Put the metal type in a wooden frame.

❹ Lift the printed paper out and hang it up to dry.

_____ → _____ → _____ → _____

C Choose the best answer to each question.

❶ What was the very first thing printed on a Gutenberg Press?

a) a German poem

b) a Latin schoolbook

c) the bible

d) a church songbook

❷ Where are the Gutenberg Bibles today?

a) They are in museums or university library collections.

b) They are owned by private collectors.

c) They are owned by insurance companies that keep them safe.

d) They are owned by banks and kept in vaults.

D Mark T for true or F for false.

❶ The Gutenberg Press allowed the spread of new ideas during the Renaissance.   T F

❷ The Gutenberg Press made printing books much faster.   T F

❸ The Gutenberg Press prevented the Scientific Revolution.   T F

Move to the Back of the Bus

White Forward, Colored Rear

The tired woman lifted her bag as she climbed the steps onto a bus in Montgomery, Alabama. She gave the driver a few coins for her fare.

On the bus was a sign that read, "White forward, colored rear." The sign was clipped on a seat a few rows back in the bus. Only white people could sit in front of the sign at the front of the bus. Black people had to sit behind the sign.

Rosa Parks sat down in the first row reserved for blacks and placed her bag on her lap.

POP QUIZ

Where did Rosa Parks sit on the bus?
ⓐ in the first row reserved for white people
ⓑ in the first row reserved for black people

▲ a "Blacks Only" water fountain,
an example of racial segregation in the U.S.

(Russell Lee [Public domain], via Wikimedia Commons)

KEY WORDS

- fare
- forward
- colored
- rear
- clip
- reserve

The bus stopped and picked up more passengers. The white section filled up. At the next stop a white man got onto the bus. He had broad shoulders and a broad smile. He joked with the bus driver as he paid his fare, and then turned to find a seat. He noticed the woman in the first black row, and the smile melted from his face.

"Hey, Mr. Blake," he said to the bus driver. "There's no more room up front in the white section."

The bus driver looked in the mirror and saw that the white man was right. With a sigh, Mr. Blake walked down the aisle. He moved the sign further back a couple of rows.

"You all are going to have to move," he told the four black people sitting in Rosa's row.

POP QUIZ

What was the bus driver's name?

ⓐ Mr. Blake   ⓑ Mr. Green

KEY WORDS

- pick up
- passenger
- fill up
- stop
- get onto (↔ get off)

- broad smile
- joke with
- notice
- melt
- room

- up front
- sigh
- aisle
- further

Three of the people moved further back in the bus. Rosa moved, but she did not move back. She moved to the window seat in the same row.

"You don't have no business sitting here," Mr. Blake said to her. Rosa looked up at the bus driver, then turned her face away and looked out the window. She didn't say a word.

Mr. Blake didn't like that. He was used to black people following orders from him. After all, he was a white man. Also, as a bus driver, he was allowed to enforce the segregation law on buses.

"Perhaps you didn't hear me," he said.

"Oh, I heard you alright," Rosa answered.

She didn't turn her face away from the window as she spoke.

"Just like I heard you that time you made me get off the bus to enter from the back door. Then you drove off and left me standing at the bus stop."

The people in the seat behind her shifted uncomfortably as Mr. Blake's face began to turn a shade of angry red. A few weeks earlier, he had played a mean joke on Rosa. Now he knew Rosa had not forgotten it.

POP QuIz

What mean joke had Mr. Blake recently played on Rosa Parks?

ⓐ He told her he wouldn't let black people ride on his bus any more.

ⓑ He drove away and left her standing at the bus stop.

KEY WORDS

- **alright** (= all right)
- **drive off** (drive-drove-driven)
- **shift**

- **uncomfortably**
- **shade**
- **play a joke on** + *Person*

"If you don't want to cause trouble, then I'd advise you to move on to the back of the bus."

Now Rosa turned and looked him right in the eyes.

"Why should I?" she asked.

"Because he's a white man, that's why. He's entitled to this here seat in the front of the bus. Your seat is in the back." Mr. Blake's nostrils flared as he tried to keep his voice calm.

"You mean to tell me that because his skin is a different color than mine he gets to choose where he sits and I do not?"

The bus driver pointed to the seats further back.

"You know the answer to that."

Rosa Parks lifted her chin and squared her shoulders.

"Yes, I do, and it is not right. So I am not moving. Not one inch."

"Mrs. Parks," he said gently. "We don't want no trouble here. Just stand up and move to the back of the bus like you're supposed to do."

Rosa Parks' eyes widened behind her glasses. "No. I am not moving."

"Then I will have to call the police." Mr. Blake waited for Rosa to move.

Rosa remained in her seat. "You may do that," she told him. Aha!

KEY WORDS

- look + *Person* + right in the eyes
- be entitled to + *Noun*[*Verb*] (*cf.* entitle)
- nostril
- flare
- get to + *Verb*

- square
- inch (= 2.54 cm)
- be supposed to + *Verb*
- widen
- remain

The bus driver went back to his seat and called the police.
When the police arrived, Rosa still refused to move. She raised
her arm and pointed her finger to the white men around her.
"They are not moving," she told them. "I am not moving."
Soon Rosa Parks was being escorted off the bus and into jail.
What had she done wrong?

Early Days of Rosa Parks

Rosa Louise McCauley was a quiet and respectful daughter of a school teacher and a carpenter. Her mother always encouraged her to get an education. This was not an easy thing for a young black woman in the 1920s in the state of Alabama. White people and black people were treated differently. They had different churches,

▲ (See page for author [Public domain], via Wikimedia Commons)

different schools, and even different drinking fountains.

▲ Even hospital waiting rooms were segregated between blacks and whites.

▲ a "Blacks Only" school
(By Mennonite Church USA Archives [No restrictions], via Wikimedia Commons)

KEY WORDS

- refuse
- raise
- escort
- jail
- respectful
- carpenter
- encourage
- drinking fountain

This racism was made even worse by the Ku Klux Klan, also called the KKK. 🌐 They used violence to scare black people and to prevent them from protesting the unfair laws. 📖

When Rosa was a teenager, her mother became ill and she had to drop out of school to take care of her. Later, she met Raymond Parks. He was a barber in Montgomery, Alabama.

KEY WORDS

- racism
- violence
- prevent from
- protest
- unfair (↔ fair)
- teenager
- become ill (become-became-become)
- drop out of school

- take care of
- barber
- diploma
- get away with
- valued
- prove
- equally (cf. equal)

They were married in 1932. As her husband, he encouraged her to finish high school. So Rosa went back to school and got her diploma.

Raymond and Rosa did not think racism was right. Rosa watched as white people got away with treating black people as if they were not valued. She saw white people beat black people, and saw signs that said "Coloreds Only" or "Whites Only." Rosa wanted to prove that everyone should be treated equally.

On December 1, 1955, Rosa Parks had had enough of the racism.  She made a stand by sitting on the bus in the place reserved for white people.

After she was arrested, Rosa Parks was ordered to pay a fine of $10 for breaking a law about segregation. Rosa said she would not pay. She said she wanted the courts to decide if the law was fair.

▲ (By Speedoflight, via Wikimedia Commons)

POP QUIZ
How much was Rosa's fine?
ⓐ $10
ⓑ $20

KEY WORDS

- have had enough (of)
- make a stand
- arrest
- fine

- **break** (break-broke-broken)
- **court**
- **decide**

Dr. Martin Luther King Jr. heard about Rosa's situation.  He gathered the black community together to protest what had happened to her. They agreed to boycott the Montgomery buses. This meant that they would no longer ride the buses to and from work, or anywhere else. This would be hard on the city, but it was even harder for the African-American citizens.

▲ Dr. Martin Luther King Jr.
(By Nobel Foundation (http://nobelprize.org/)
[Public domain or Public domain],
via Wikimedia Commons)

POP QUIZ

What is the meaning of the word "boycott"?
ⓐ to buy or use
ⓑ not to buy or use

KEY WORDS

- gather
- community

- happen to
- boycott

- no longer
- citizen

Most of them did not own cars. To get to work without the bus, many people had to walk, ride bicycles, or ride in a carpool. Some of them even began using horse drawn carts! African-American taxi drivers lowered their fares to ten cents. That was the same price as a bus ride. Even though it was hard to do, the black community united and boycotted the Montgomery buses for more than a year! The boycott lasted 381 days. It finally ended when the Supreme Court decided that the segregation laws in Alabama were wrong.

The boycott made many white people angry at the civil rights leaders. The government started making taxi drivers pay a fine if they didn't charge at least 45 cents.

Rosa Parks was threatened and fired from her job as a seamstress. Other black people were attacked. Dr. Martin Luther King Jr.'s house was bombed. Even through all of this, he preached for peace.

KEY WORDS

- carpool
- cart
- lower
- last

- the Supreme Court
- civil rights
- at least
- threaten

- fire
- seamstress
- bomb
- preach

More Work for Rosa

Rosa and Raymond decided to move to Detroit, Michigan in 1957. During her years in Detroit, Rosa Parks never stopped

fighting for civil rights. She worked as the secretary for U.S. Representative John Conyers. 🌐 Together they fought for equal treatment for everyone. Rosa was especially active in helping black women who had been abused by white men.

▲ John Conyers
(By US Government Printing Office
(Pictorial Directory, 95th US Congress, p. 71)
[Public domain], via Wikimedia Commons)

KEY WORDS

- secretary
- **Representative** (*cf.* representative)
- especially
- active
- abuse
- icon
- **look up to** (= respect)
- bravery

- congressional
- presidential
- **fly at half-mast** (fly-flew-flown)
  (*cf.* half-mast)
- throughout
- humble
- quote

Over the years, she became an icon for civil rights. People looked up to her for her bravery in fighting things that are wrong. She even received the Congressional Gold Medal and the Presidential Medal of Freedom. These are both high awards. On the day of her funeral in 2005, President George Bush ordered

that all the flags in the United States should be flown at half-mast.

Throughout her life, Rosa remained humble.

She said in a famous quote, "I would like to be remembered as a person who wanted to be free… so other people would be also free."

POP QUIZ

What happened on the day of Rosa's funeral in 2005?

ⓐ All flags in the nation were lowered to half-mast.

ⓑ There were parades for her in many big cities.

Comprehension Quiz

A Fill in each blank with the right word(s) below.

segregation	civil rights	Representative	bombed

❶ Rosa Parks is admired for her bravery in fighting for the
_____ of all people.

❷ Martin Luther King Jr.'s house was _____.

❸ Bus drivers collected fares and enforced the _____ law.

❹ Rosa Parks was a secretary for United States _____
John Conyers.

B Mark T for true or F for false.

❶ The Montgomery bus boycott lasted for 38 months. ⬛T ⬛F

❷ The Supreme Court decided the segregation laws in
Alabama were wrong. ⬛T ⬛F

❸ Rosa wanted to be remembered as a person who
wanted to be free. ⬛T ⬛F

❹ On Rosa's birthdays, all flags in the nation were
lowered to half-mast. ⬛T ⬛F

C Choose the best answer to each question.

❶ What did Rosa Parks do when she was asked to move?

a) She stood up and said, "No way."

b) She stayed in her row and moved to a window seat.

c) She asked a white man to help her move her bag.

d) She pretended she was asleep because she was tired.

❷ Why did Rosa have to drop out of school?

a) Her parents were too poor to send her to school.

b) The other students at school were mean to her.

c) The law said black people could not go to school.

d) Her mother became ill and she had to take care of her.

❸ What are two of the many awards Rosa Parks has received?

a) Caldecott Medal

b) Coretta Scott King Award

c) Congressional Gold Medal

d) Presidential Medal of Freedom

Tear Down This Wall

Christmas 1989 was a special day in Berlin. It was like no other Christmas that had ever happened before.

▲ Brandenburg Gate

An orchestra performed at the Brandenburg Gate in Berlin. The classical song by Beethoven, "Ode to Joy" rang out from their instruments. But instead of the word "joy," they called it "freedom." As the beautiful music floated through the air, people hugged and cried and celebrated. At the same time, they were destroying a huge wall around the city. Why? What were the people celebrating?

KEY WORDS

- **tear down** (tear-tore-torn)
- **perform**
- **ode**
- **ring out** (ring-rang-rung)

- **instrument** (= musical instrument)
- **float**
- **hug**
- **at the same time**

▲ a checkpoint sign near the Berlin Wall

From August 1961 until November 1989, a twelve-foot-high wall separated West Berlin from East Germany and East Berlin. People in East Berlin were not allowed to leave and go to West Berlin. They were in prison in their own city. Many people tried to escape. Some made it out, while others died trying. But on November 9, 1989, all that changed. Crowds gathered at the main gate, the Brandenburg Gate. People took out sledgehammers and began chipping away at the wall. The wall was coming down! As they worked, a famous band called Crosby, Stills & Nash played the song, "Chippin' Away."

KEY WORDS

- separate
- make it out
- while
- main gate
- sledgehammer

- chip away at
- come down
- party
- shake hands with (shake-shook-shaken)
- guard

This was only the beginning of tearing down the wall. For a year, the celebrations continued. On New Year's Eve, David Hasselhoff stood on top of the wall and sang "Looking for Freedom." People partied and hugged as they continued tearing down the wall. In places where there was a hole in the wall, people reached through and shook hands with guards on the other side.

This was an important time in history. It symbolized the fall of Communism in the Soviet Union. It opened a new way of life for the people who had lived behind the wall for so many years. It was the start of a new relationship between Russia and the United States.

After World War II in 1945, Germany was a divided nation. The western part of Germany had a democratic government and eastern part had a communist government. These two different ideologies, or belief systems, also created what was known as the Cold War.  No bombs were dropped, no battles were fought. The war was about what type of government was the best.

POP QUIZ

Mark T for true or F for false.

After World War II, the eastern part of Germany had a communist government.   **T / F**

KEY WORDS

- symbolize
- communism
- divided

- democratic
- communist
- ideology

- belief
- Cold War

The city of Berlin like the rest of Germany had been divided into four zones controlled by different countries. Great Britain, France, and the United States controlled West Berlin. The Soviet Union controlled East Berlin. The problem was Berlin itself was completely surrounded by East Germany.

KEY WORDS

▪ zone

▪ control

West Germany had plenty of food and clothing, and the people had a great deal of freedom under democratic government. In East Germany, there were often shortages of food, clothing, and other supplies. People did not have freedom of speech or other freedoms. To escape these conditions, East Germans entered West Berlin. There they were free to go to the western countries. Many of the people leaving were well educated teachers, doctors, and engineers. The communist government did not want to lose these people.

So they created a special secret project. On the night of August 12, 1961, West Berliners went to sleep just as they normally did. When they awoke the next morning, there was a barbed wire fence being put up all around their city. East German soldiers guarded the fence with guns. They were under orders not to let anyone go through the fence. They closed the main gate, the Brandenburg Gate. Soviet and East German tanks patrolled the city limits.

KEY WORDS

- plenty of
- a great deal of (= a lot of)
- shortage
- educated

- normally
- awake (awake-awoke-awoken)
- barbed wire
- put up (put-put-put)

- under orders
- tank
- patrol
- limits (= boundary)

As the days and months went by, the East Germans put
concrete blocks up to 12 feet high into the wall to stop people
from leaving. Eventually, the wall was over 100 miles long.
But even a wall of this size couldn't stop people from trying to
escape to freedom.

KEY WORDS

- go by
- concrete

- eventually
- stop + *Person* + from + *Verb*-ing

People were very creative in thinking of ways to get past the wall.  Some people sewed silk together and made hot air balloons. When that happened, the East Germans made silk and other lightweight fabrics illegal. Some people used ropes to climb the walls. Then the East Germans made rope illegal. A tunnel was dug from a bakery in West Berlin to an outhouse in East Berlin. It was found and destroyed. Other people tried to swim across rivers or jump over the wall.

KEY WORDS

- get past
- hot air balloon
- lightweight
- fabric

- illegal (↔ legal)
- dig (dig-dug-dug)
- outhouse

On a street called Harzer Strasse there was a four-story apartment building.  The street was in West Berlin, but the apartment building was in East Berlin. Some people jumped out of the windows of the apartment building and landed on the street in West Berlin. After this, the East German soldiers nailed all the windows and doors shut on that side of the building. Then they made brick walls out of the windows and doors. They turned the building into part of the Berlin Wall.

KEY WORDS

- story
- land
- nail
- shut (shut-shut-shut)
- watchtower
- be filled with

- land mine
- trip wire
- gravel
- strip
- lose one's life (lose-lost-lost)

The Berlin Wall had more than 300 watchtowers. Guards were ordered to shoot and kill anyone trying to climb the wall. One area was filled with land mines and trip wires. It was a gravel strip called the "death strip." 🌐 This area separated the buildings in East Berlin and the wall. Anyone trying to escape from here had to cross the "death strip." Over 200 people lost their lives trying to escape from East Germany.

▲ death strip

(GeorgeLouis at English Wikipedia [GFDL (http://www.gnu.org/copyleft/fdl.html) or CC BY-SA 3.0 (http://creativecommons.org/licenses/by-sa/3.0)], via Wikimedia Commons)

New Days for Freedom

▲ Mikhail Gorbachev
(RIA Novosti archive, image # / CC-BY-SA 3.0
[CC BY-SA 3.0 (http://creativecommons.org/
licenses/by-sa/3.0) or CC BY-SA 3.0 (http://
creativecommons.org/licenses/by-sa/3.0)],
via Wikimedia Commons)

In 1985 a new leader named Mikhail Gorbachev became the chairman of the Soviet Union. 🌐 He wanted to become friendly with democratic countries. He made new policies for the Russian government. One was called "glasnost" which means openness. Another was called "perestroika" which means democratic reform or restructuring.

KEY WORDS

- chairman
- policy
- glasnost
- openness
- perestroika

- reform
- restructuring
- **make a speech** (make-made-made)
- **start a riot** (*cf.* riot)

President Ronald Reagan worked for peace between the Soviet Union and the United States. In 1987, he made a famous speech at the Brandenburg Gate in West Berlin.

In his speech he said, "Mr. Chairman, tear down this wall!"

▲ (By White House photographer [Public domain], via Wikimedia Commons)

People in East Berlin became angrier and angrier about the wall.

In 1987 a famous rock star named David Bowie went to West Berlin. He had lived in Germany and the people loved his music. During his concert, people on the East Berlin side started a riot.

Then Bruce Springsteen played a concert in 1988 in East Berlin. He told the people, "I hope one day the barriers will be torn down."

Over the next two years, more riots happened as people grew more and more tired of the wall.

On November 9, 1989, it was announced that the people of East Berlin could now travel to the West. During a press conference, a spokesman read a message that said the gates to the West would be opened.

The interviewer asked, "When will this happen?"

▲ a picture of the press conference
that led to the fall of the Berlin Wall

(Bundesarchiv, Bild 183-1989-1109-030 / Lehmann, Thomas / CC-BY-SA 3.0 [CC BY-SA 3.0 de (http://creativecommons.org/licenses/by-sa/3.0/de/deed.en)], via Wikimedia Commons)

The spokesman read his note again. Then he said, "Immediately."

KEY WORDS

- barrier
- announce
- press conference (*cf.* conference)
- spokesman
- interviewer

- note
- immediately
- yell at
- thousands of
- pour

- chisel
- pickax
- break off
- nickname
- woodpecker

People raced to different places along the wall. They yelled at the guards, "Open the gates!"

Others climbed up on top of the wall. The guards were forced to open the gates. On November 10, thousands of people poured through Brandenburg Gate to celebrate freedom. Some of them used sledgehammers, chisels, hammers, and pickaxes to break off pieces of the wall. These people were nicknamed "Wall Woodpeckers."

Large pieces of the wall were sent to museums and memorials around the world. Small pieces were sold as souvenirs to help people remember this day of freedom. The pieces from the east side of the wall are plain gray. The guards on the east side never allowed anyone to get near the wall or to touch it. The people on the west side had freedom of speech and expression and they covered the wall with graffiti about freedom. Today, if you see a piece of the wall, that is how you can tell which side faced East Berlin and which side faced West Berlin.

▲ a piece of the Berlin Wall in the Ronald Reagan Presidential Library
(Courtesy Ronald Reagan Library [Attribution], via Wikimedia Commons)

KEY WORDS

- memorial
- souvenir

- plain
- graffiti (*cf.* graffito)

- face

▲ an photograph of graffiti on the Berlin Wall

Comprehension Quiz

A Match each person[people] with the correct explanation.

❶ Ronald Reagan •

❷ Wall Woodpeckers •

❸ Mikhail Gorbachev •

• a) a former leader of the Soviet Union

• b) people who chipped away at the Berlin Wall

• c) a U.S. president who worked for peace between the Soviet Union and the United States

B Fill in each blank with the right word below.

limits	memorials	shortages	barriers

❶ In East Germany, there were often _____ of food, clothing, and other supplies.

❷ Soviet and East German tanks patrolled the city _____.

❸ Bruce Springsteen told the people, "I hope one day the _____ will be torn down."

❹ Large pieces of the wall were sent to museums and _____ around the world.

C Choose the best answer to each question.

❶ How big was the Berlin Wall?

a) In some places it was twelve feet high.

b) It was eight feet high.

c) It was 200 miles long.

d) In some places it was twenty feet high.

❷ How did East Germany turn the apartment building into a portion of the Berlin Wall?

a) They tore down the building and used the bricks to build the wall.

b) They built brick walls inside all the doors and windows that faced Harzer Strasse.

c) They hammered wooden boards over the doors and windows.

d) They put bars on all the doors and windows.

D Put the sentences in order.

❶ David Bowie gives a concert.

❷ The barbed wire fence is erected.

❸ The wall comes down.

❹ The Soviet Union gets a new chairman.

_____ → _____ → _____ → _____

Let's Review the Story

Fill in the blanks to review the story.

Title: Turning [_____] in World History

The Mongol Wars

As a young man, Genghis Khan went by the name [T___]. He wanted to [u___] the Mongol [t___]. After conquering vast lands, he created the [G___] [L___] of Genghis Khan. He set up a [m___] service between tribes. He created a [w___] language. He invented strategies for [w___] that are still used today.

Million Dollar Bibles

Johannes Gutenberg is credited with the invention of [m___] [t___]. His press used metal type in a [w___] frame, [i___] balls to spread the ink, and a [p___] to press the ink onto the paper. He printed about 200 [G___] [B___] using his press. His invention led to the Age of [E___].

Move to the Back of the Bus

Rosa Parks is an icon for [c___] [r___]. She refused to move to the back of the [b___] because she knew all people should have [e___] rights. This started the Montgomery bus [b___]. Rosa spent many years working for civil rights with U.S. Representative John Conyers. She received the Presidential [M___] of [F___].

Tear Down This Wall

In August of 1961 East [G___] built a wall around West [B___] to keep East Germans from going to the West. The government of East Germany controlled East Berlin and was [c___] while West Berlin was democratic and controlled by West Germany. This difference of ideologies was called the [C___] [W___]. President Ronald Reagan asked the Soviet leader to tear down the [w___]. In November of 1989 the wall came down. Pieces of the wall were sent around the world to [r___] this day of freedom.

Let's Think & Talk

Think about the following questions and answer them freely.

❶ How did Genghis Khan and Rosa Park become important historical figures? Tell us what they did.

❷ How did Gutenberg's printing press and the fall of the Berlin Wall influence history? Tell us how people's lives have changed by comparing life before and after these events.

❸ In the book, which person or event do you think had the most important influence on history? Why?

❹ Besides the stories in the book, do you know any important historical figures or events? Why do you think they are important?

Let's Review the Story

Title: Turning   Points   in World History

The Mongol Wars

As a young man, Genghis Khan went by the name Temüjin . He wanted to unite the Mongol tribes . After conquering vast lands, he created the Great   Law of Genghis Khan. He set up a mail service between tribes. He created a written language. He invented strategies for war that are still used today.

Million Dollar Bibles

Johannes Gutenberg is credited with the invention of movable   type . His press used metal type in a wooden frame, ink balls to spread the ink, and a platen to press the ink onto the paper. He printed about 200 Gutenberg   Bibles using his press. His invention led to the Age of Enlightenment .

Move to the Back of the Bus

Rosa Parks is an icon for civil   rights . She refused to move to the back of the bus because she knew all people should have equal rights. This started the Montgomery bus boycott . Rosa spent many years working for civil rights with U.S. Representative John Conyers. She received the Presidential Medal of Freedom .

Tear Down This Wall

In August of 1961 East Germany built a wall around West Berlin to keep East Germans from going to the West. The government of East Germany controlled East Berlin and was communist while West Berlin was democratic and controlled by West Germany. This difference of ideologies was called the Cold   War . President Ronald Reagan asked the Soviet leader to tear down the wall . In November of 1989 the wall came down. Pieces of the wall were sent around the world to remember this day of freedom.

Smart Readers: **Wise & Wide**

After-reading **Test**

- **Turning Points in World History**
- **Level 5**
- **27 Questions**

(Vocabulary 5 / Reading Comprehension 16 /

Sentence Structure & Grammar 6)

1. What does "steppe" mean?
   ① a part of a ladder
   ② a grassland
   ③ a small forest
   ④ a mountainous area

2. What does "vellum" mean?
   ① flaxen paper
   ② animal skins used as paper
   ③ bamboo paper
   ④ rice paper

3. Which of the following is the wrong past tense form of the verb?
   ① sewed
   ② rode
   ③ leapt
   ④ digged

4. Which of the following is similar to the word below?

   > Gutenberg Bibles are <u>prized</u> documents.

   ① difficult to find
   ② common
   ③ cheap
   ④ valuable

5. What is the common word for the two blanks?

> • How did Gutenberg come up _____ this idea for printing with movable type?
> • However, Gutenberg is credited _____ inventing a new technique and introducing the printing technology to Europe.

① to   ② with
③ from   ④ by

6. Why were Temüjin and his family cast out of their clan?
① Temüjin killed someone in the clan.
② Temüjin wanted to move back to his own clan.
③ Temüjin's father was dead and his mother was an outsider.
④ Temüjin broke a rule about stealing.

7. When Börte was kidnapped, what did Temüjin do?
① He went into the woods and cried.
② He joined with Toghril, Jamuka, and 40,000 men to rescue her.
③ He made an altar in her memory.
④ He followed the kidnappers and silently snuck into their camp.

8. Why did Jamuka attack Temüjin's tribe after they had been *andas*?
① Jamuka was jealous because Temüjin was rich.
② Jamuka and Temüjin had an argument over a woman.
③ Jamuka wanted to punish Temüjin's tribe for a kidnapping.
④ Jamuka was jealous because Temüjin had been named the Mongol leader.

9. What was the tumbleweed formation?
   ① Soldiers attacked the enemy from many different directions.
   ② Soldiers hid behind bushes and lit the bushes on fire.
   ③ Soldiers rolled tumbleweeds in front of them as they advanced on the enemy.
   ④ Soldiers rode like the wind around the enemy camp.

10. How were books made before the Gutenberg Press? Choose two answers.
    ① They were copied by hand.
    ② They were printed using woodcarvings.
    ③ They were sent to China and printed there.
    ④ They were printed using rubber stamps.

11. Why didn't everyone learn to read before the Gutenberg Press?
    ① Books were too expensive for most people to buy.
    ② People were not as smart as they are today.
    ③ People had to work all the time and didn't have time to read.
    ④ They only needed to read if they worked for a printer.

12. What time periods in history are NOT credited in part to the Gutenberg Press?
    ① the Scientific Revolution
    ② the Reformation
    ③ the Industrial Revolution
    ④ the Age of Enlightenment

13. What did the sign on the Montgomery bus say?

① White forward, colored rear.

② Please wear your seat belt.

③ No air conditioning.

④ Cash only.

14. What did Mr. Blake finally do when Rosa wouldn't move to the back of the bus?

① He picked her up and carried her off the bus.

② He contacted the police.

③ He threw her bag off the bus.

④ He took away her bus pass.

15. What did the black community do in support of Rosa Parks?

① They raised money to help pay her fine.

② They organized a boycott of the Montgomery buses.

③ They staged a protest at the White House.

④ They stopped going to their jobs.

16. What did Rosa Parks and Representative Conyers want?

① They wanted to sue the police for taking Rosa to jail.

② They wanted to start a college for black people.

③ They wanted equal treatment for everyone.

④ They wanted to close the Montgomery bus service.

17. What was the Cold War?
   ① It was a war in the middle of a very cold winter.
   ② It was a war that was in Sweden and Denmark.
   ③ It was a war without battles to decide whether democracy or communism was best.
   ④ It was a war to release prisoners from a prison with no heat.

18. What country controlled East Berlin?
   ① Norway
   ② the Soviet Union
   ③ United States
   ④ France

19. Why did people want to leave East Berlin and East Germany? Choose two answers.
   ① There were shortages of food and supplies.
   ② The weather was nicer in West Berlin.
   ③ West Berlin had better schools.
   ④ They did not have freedom.

20. Why did people jump out the windows of the apartment building on Harzer Strasse?
   ① The people were bungee jumping.
   ② The apartment building caught on fire.
   ③ The other side of the street was West Berlin and freedom.
   ④ The people were jumping onto trampolines.

21. What was the death strip along the Berlin Wall?

① It was a barren strip of land with no rainfall.

② It was a road that led to Death Valley.

③ It was a road that led to the prison camps.

④ It was a gravel area filled with trip wires and land mines.

※ Choose the wrong part of each sentence. (22~23)

22.
They used violence to scare black people and to prevent them from
                                   ①   ②   ③

protest the unfair laws.
④

23.
He learned to ride a horse and shoot a bow and arrow as soon as
             ①   ②

his legs were enough long to reach the stirrups.
             ③   ④

※ Choose the correct sentence. (24~25)

24. ① No one know with certain.

② No one knows to certain.

③ No one knows for certain.

④ No one know by certain.

25. ① You have no business sitting here.

② You don't have no business sit here.

③ You don't have business to sitting here.

④ You don't have no business to have sit here.

※ Choose the correct word or phrase for each blank. (26~27)

26.

Around 1455 Johannes printed almost 200 copies of _____ the Gutenberg Bible.

① calling

② let it call

③ what we call

④ having called

27.

It covered nearly _____ of the continent of Asia.

① four one

② one four

③ fourth one

④ one fourth

Suzanne Pitner

Suzanne Pitner is a teacher and writer who has enjoyed visiting Alaska, exploring Rome, teaching in China, and is looking forward to more world travel. She has a Master's Degree in Education, and is a graduate of the Long Ridge Writer's Group. In addition to writing educational articles and books, she writes historical fiction and contemporary fiction for young adults using the pen name Suzanne Lilly.

 Smart Readers Wise & Wide 5-10

Turning Points in World History

Written by Suzanne Pitner
Illustrated by Yeonjo Kim

First Published in November 2017

Editorial Manager: Juyon Choi
Editors: Kyunghee Jang, Myungjin Kim, Jiyeong Park
Designers: Eunhee Lee, Elim
Cover Designer: Eunhee Lee

Published and distributed by

 Happy House

Darakwon Bldg., 64-1 Jandari-ro, Mapo-gu, Seoul, Korea 04031
Tel: 82-2-736-2031(ext. 250)   Fax: 82-2-732-2037
Homepage: www.ihappyhouse.co.kr
Publisher: Kyudo Chung

Copyright © Darakwon Publishing Company 2017
English Edition published 2017, by arrangement with Darakwon, by Happy House
English Edition Copyright © 2017, Happy House

All rights reserved. No part of this publication may be reproduced, stored in
a retrieval system, or transmitted in any form or by any means, electronic,
mechanical, photocopying or otherwise, without the prior consent of the
copyright owner. Refund after purchase is possible only according to the company
regulations. Contact the above telephone number for any inquiries.
Consumer damages caused by loss, damage, etc. can be compensated
according to the consumer dispute resolution standards announced by the Korea
Fair Trade Commission. An incorrectly collated book will be exchanged.

ISBN: 978-89-6653-551-4 18740 / 978-89-6653-156-1 18740(set)

[Components]
• 1 Audio CD (Recording Studio: Aram)
• Answer Keys & Korean Translation: Free download at www.ihappyhouse.co.kr

Image Credit: shutterstock.com / Wikimedia Commons